Prayer Journal

6 MONTHS OF PRAYER, SCRIPTURE AND GRATITUDE

_____

Psalms 119:105

Your word is a lamp for my feet, a light on my path.

I really want to thank you for buying this book. I've prepared something special. If you would like to receive print-ready planning cards to help you establish good habits and achieve your goals, see the page 206 of this journal.

LET'S STAY IN CONTACT!

 infoevendiem@gmail.com

instagram.com/evendiem/

I know you're probably busy, but if you would like to take a minute of your precious time to share your opinion about this journal on Amazon, I would be truly grateful. It's worth more than gold to me. You contribute to the improvement of the quality of this book.

Thank you in advance.

Scan the QR code with your phone's camera and share your opinion

Table of Contents

5

WELCOME

5

HOW TO USE THIS JOURNAL?

6

SHORT INSTRUCTION

8

31 DAYS OF LOVE FOR GOD AND NEIGHBOR

41

31 DAYS OF GOD'S LOVE

74

31 DAYS OF FORGIVENESS

107

31 DAYS OF FAITH AND HOPE

140

31 DAYS OF HEALING: HOW TO SURVIVE IN THE TOUGHEST TIMES?

173

31 DAYS OF GENTLENESS AND PATIENCE

206

GIFT

207

NOTES

Hello,

I am very glad that you decided to buy this Prayer Journal. It will undoubtedly change your relationship with God and other people. Praying, expressing gratitude and reading the Scriptures are essential elements of the Christian life.

Daily reflection and prayer will bring you relief in difficult times, as well as true happiness and joy in the most beautiful ones. This journal will help you find yourself, survive your grief, and show you in which direction you should go. However, the rest is in the hands of the Father. Therefore, take at least 5 minutes a day to complete this journal. These 5 minutes are your conversation with the Father, which we must not forget, because it is thanks to Him that we live.

I hope this journal will make your life fuller and bring you closer to God and your prayers will be heard. I wish you all the best on your path of faith.

Even Diem

How to use this journal?

There is no single method on how to use this journal. You can customize it according to your needs. You do not have to stick to the order of topics, but choose the one you need the most at the moment and continue it for 31 days. Treat these daily notes as talking to God and as a prayer and a wonderful habit worth cultivating.

When it comes to keeping a diary on a daily basis, there are many options. I will introduce you to 2 of them. However, there is no obstacle to choosing your own:

- You can start your day by writing things for which you are thankful. Then during the day, take a moment to write a reflection on a Bible quote, and at the end of the day, write down your request to God.

- You can also just do these three things at once, right after you wake up or at night before going to bed or when you have a moment during the day. Decide as you prefer and stick to your resolution.

Short instruction

"For every house is built by someone, but God is the builder of everything."

Hebrews 3:4

② MY LORD, I AM THANKFUL FOR

- a beautiful morning with my family
- health and strength
- my friends I can rely on
- I am grateful to have a place to live.

③ REFLECTIONS & THOUGHTS

Today's words from the Bible especially emphasize your majesty, Father. You created it all and it is thanks to you that we live. Everything I have belongs to you. The house would be empty without you, because you make sense of everything in my life. Sometimes I forget that in fact all material goods are nothing compared to what I get from You. I am sorry that I am often so busy and I don't see the beauty of the world that you have built.

Lord, you are with me and you take care of everything, teach me to build, not to ruin.

④ PRAYER REQUEST

Lord, please help me make the right decision in tomorrow's meeting. You know what I need and what is best for me.
I'm asking for health and care for my whole family.
Make my faith grow stronger every day.

(1) QUOTE FROM THE BIBLE
Inspirational and the most beautiful verses.

(2) MY LORD, I AM THANKFUL FOR
Express your gratitude every day.

(3) REFLECTIONS & THOUGHTS
Place for your reflections on a Bible quote. Write down everything you feel in your heart. Think about what you can learn from this verse and how it affects your life. What is God trying to tell you?

(4) PRAYER REQUEST
What would you like to ask God for?

- Each new chapter begins with a verse from the Bible and a short introduction and description.

- Then there is space for your thoughts and reflections on the chapter and verse.

- If you need more space for your reflections, see the back of this journal.

If you go through all the topics, I encourage you to come back to your thoughts, requests and thanks. I can assure you that you can discover something special in these wonderful words from the Bible each time.

Make this prayer journal your personal guide to the Lord.

31 DAYS OF LOVE FOR GOD AND NEIGHBOR

"Love is patient, love is kind. It does not envy, it does not boast, it is not proud. It is not rude, it is not self-seeking, it is not easily angered, it keeps no record of wrongs. Love does not delight in evil but rejoices with the truth. It always protects, always trusts, always hopes, always perseveres. Love never fails."

1 Corinthians 13:4-8

Love is present in our lives from an early age and everyone, regardless of age, encounters this feeling in various forms. It can be parental, brotherly, friendly or marital love. Many have tried to define what love really is, and there is no clear answer to this, but the statements that love is nothing more than the desire for good and the basic source of human happiness seem to be extremely accurate. Love is a gift we have received from God and should be cared for. God wants us to love our neighbor as He loves us - unconditionally and selflessly. Jan Twardowski said "We still love too little and still too late" - often these words turn out to be true. We should take care of love every day, even and maybe especially when it is difficult and when we no longer have the strength and will. So, read this verse from the Bible several times, come back to it, and share this wonderful love with others as God shares it with us. Use this time well for reflection, conversations with God and with your neighbors. Let your life be filled to the brim with the purest and most beautiful LOVE.

MY THOUGHTS

DAY AND DATE _____ ___/___/_____

> "Do everything in love."

1 Corinthians 16:14

MY LORD, I AM THANKFUL FOR

_____
_____
_____
_____
_____

REFLECTIONS & THOUGHTS

_____
_____
_____
_____
_____
_____
_____
_____
_____
_____
_____

PRAYER REQUEST

_____
_____
_____
_____
_____

DAY AND DATE _____ ___/___/_____

MY LORD, I AM THANKFUL FOR

_____

_____

_____

_____

REFLECTIONS & THOUGHTS

_____

_____

_____

_____

_____

_____

_____

_____

_____

_____

_____

PRAYER REQUEST

_____

_____

_____

_____

> "Greater love has no one than this: to lay down one's life for one's friends."

John 15:13

MY LORD, I AM THANKFUL FOR

_____

_____

_____

_____

_____

REFLECTIONS & THOUGHTS

_____

_____

_____

_____

_____

_____

_____

_____

_____

_____

_____

_____

PRAYER REQUEST

_____

_____

_____

_____

DAY AND DATE _____ ___/___/_____

MY LORD, I AM THANKFUL FOR

_____

_____

_____

_____

REFLECTIONS & THOUGHTS

_____

_____

_____

_____

_____

_____

_____

_____

_____

_____

PRAYER REQUEST

_____

_____

_____

_____

"May the Lord make your love increase and overflow for each other and for everyone else, just as ours does for you."

1 Thessalonians 3:12

MY LORD, I AM THANKFUL FOR

REFLECTIONS & THOUGHTS

PRAYER REQUEST

DAY AND DATE _____ ___/___/_____

MY LORD, I AM THANKFUL FOR

_____
_____
_____
_____
_____

REFLECTIONS & THOUGHTS

_____
_____
_____
_____
_____
_____
_____
_____
_____
_____
_____

PRAYER REQUEST

_____
_____
_____
_____

DAY AND DATE _____ ___/___/___

"Whoever pursues righteousness and love finds life, prosperity and honor."

Proverbs 21:21

MY LORD, I AM THANKFUL FOR

_____
_____
_____
_____
_____

REFLECTIONS & THOUGHTS

_____
_____
_____
_____
_____
_____
_____
_____
_____
_____
_____

PRAYER REQUEST

_____
_____
_____
_____
_____

DAY AND DATE _____ ___ / ___ / ___

"The second is this: 'Love your neighbor as yourself.' There is no commandment greater than these."

Mark 12:31

MY LORD, I AM THANKFUL FOR

_____
_____
_____
_____
_____

REFLECTIONS & THOUGHTS

_____
_____
_____
_____
_____
_____
_____
_____
_____
_____
_____
_____

PRAYER REQUEST

_____
_____
_____
_____
_____

DAY AND DATE _____ ___/___/___

> "Whoever does not love does not know God, because God is love."

1 John 4:8

MY LORD, I AM THANKFUL FOR

_____
_____
_____
_____
_____

REFLECTIONS & THOUGHTS

_____
_____
_____
_____
_____
_____
_____
_____
_____
_____
_____

PRAYER REQUEST

_____
_____
_____
_____

DAY AND DATE _____ ___/___/____

MY LORD, I AM THANKFUL FOR

_____
_____
_____
_____
_____

REFLECTIONS & THOUGHTS

_____
_____
_____
_____
_____
_____
_____
_____
_____
_____
_____
_____
_____

PRAYER REQUEST

_____
_____
_____
_____

DAY AND DATE _____ ___/___/___

MY LORD, I AM THANKFUL FOR

_____
_____
_____
_____
_____

REFLECTIONS & THOUGHTS

_____
_____
_____
_____
_____
_____
_____
_____
_____
_____
_____
_____

PRAYER REQUEST

_____
_____
_____
_____
_____

DAY AND DATE _____ ___/___/_____

> "Husbands, love your wives, just as Christ loved the church and gave himself up for her to make her holy, cleansing her by the washing with water through the word."
>
> **Ephesians 5:25-26**

MY LORD, I AM THANKFUL FOR

_____
_____
_____
_____
_____

REFLECTIONS & THOUGHTS

_____
_____
_____
_____
_____
_____
_____
_____
_____
_____
_____
_____
_____

PRAYER REQUEST

_____
_____
_____
_____

"There is no fear in love. But perfect love drives out fear, because fear has to do with punishment. The one who fears is not made perfect in love."

1 John 4:18

MY LORD, I AM THANKFUL FOR

_____

_____

_____

_____

_____

REFLECTIONS & THOUGHTS

_____

_____

_____

_____

_____

_____

_____

_____

_____

_____

_____

_____

PRAYER REQUEST

_____

_____

_____

_____

_____

DAY AND DATE _____ ___/___/____

> "Finally, all of you, be like-minded, be sympathetic, love one another, be compassionate and humble."

1 Peter 3:8

MY LORD, I AM THANKFUL FOR

_____
_____
_____
_____
_____

REFLECTIONS & THOUGHTS

_____
_____
_____
_____
_____
_____
_____
_____
_____
_____
_____
_____
_____

PRAYER REQUEST

_____
_____
_____
_____
_____

DAY AND DATE _____ ___/___/____

MY LORD, I AM THANKFUL FOR

_____
_____
_____
_____
_____

REFLECTIONS & THOUGHTS

_____
_____
_____
_____
_____
_____
_____
_____
_____
_____
_____
_____

PRAYER REQUEST

_____
_____
_____
_____

DAY AND DATE _____ ___/___/_____

"For the entire law is fulfilled in keeping this one command: - Love your neighbor as yourself."

Galatians 5:14

MY LORD, I AM THANKFUL FOR

_____
_____
_____
_____

REFLECTIONS & THOUGHTS

_____
_____
_____
_____
_____
_____
_____
_____
_____
_____

PRAYER REQUEST

_____
_____
_____
_____

DAY AND DATE _____ ___/___/_____

"Carry each other's burdens, and in this way you will fulfill the law of Christ."

Galatians 6:2

MY LORD, I AM THANKFUL FOR

_____
_____
_____
_____
_____

REFLECTIONS & THOUGHTS

_____
_____
_____
_____
_____
_____
_____
_____
_____
_____
_____

PRAYER REQUEST

_____
_____
_____
_____

DAY AND DATE _____ ___/___/____

"So in everything, do to others what you would have them do to you, for this sums up the Law and the Prophets."

Matthew 7:12

MY LORD, I AM THANKFUL FOR

_____
_____
_____
_____
_____

REFLECTIONS & THOUGHTS

_____
_____
_____
_____
_____
_____
_____
_____
_____
_____
_____
_____

PRAYER REQUEST

_____
_____
_____
_____
_____

"Do nothing out of selfish ambition or vain conceit. Rather, in humility value others above yourselves."

Philippians 2:3

MY LORD, I AM THANKFUL FOR

_____
_____
_____
_____
_____

REFLECTIONS & THOUGHTS

_____
_____
_____
_____
_____
_____
_____
_____
_____
_____
_____
_____

PRAYER REQUEST

_____
_____
_____
_____
_____

DAY AND DATE _____ ___ / ___ / ____

MY LORD, I AM THANKFUL FOR

_____
_____
_____
_____

REFLECTIONS & THOUGHTS

_____
_____
_____
_____
_____
_____
_____
_____
_____
_____
_____
_____

PRAYER REQUEST

_____
_____
_____
_____

"Keep on loving one another as brothers and sisters. Do not forget to show hospitality to strangers, for by so doing some people have shown hospitality to angels without knowing it."

Hebrews 13:1-2

MY LORD, I AM THANKFUL FOR

REFLECTIONS & THOUGHTS

PRAYER REQUEST

"This is how we know what love is: Jesus Christ laid down his life for us. And we ought to lay down our lives for our brothers and sisters."

1 John 3:16

MY LORD, I AM THANKFUL FOR

REFLECTIONS & THOUGHTS

PRAYER REQUEST

DAY AND DATE _____ ___/___/___

MY LORD, I AM THANKFUL FOR

_____
_____
_____
_____
_____

REFLECTIONS & THOUGHTS

_____
_____
_____
_____
_____
_____
_____
_____
_____
_____
_____

PRAYER REQUEST

_____
_____
_____
_____

DAY AND DATE _____ ___/___/___

MY LORD, I AM THANKFUL FOR

_____
_____
_____
_____
_____

REFLECTIONS & THOUGHTS

_____
_____
_____
_____
_____
_____
_____
_____
_____
_____
_____
_____

PRAYER REQUEST

_____
_____
_____
_____

"If anyone has material possessions and sees a brother or sister in need but has no pity on them, how can the love of God be in that person?"

1 John 3:17

MY LORD, I AM THANKFUL FOR

_____

_____

_____

_____

_____

REFLECTIONS & THOUGHTS

_____

_____

_____

_____

_____

_____

_____

_____

_____

_____

_____

PRAYER REQUEST

_____

_____

_____

_____

DAY AND DATE _____ / __ / _____

> "A new command I give you: Love one another. As I have loved you, so you must love one another."

John 13:34

MY LORD, I AM THANKFUL FOR

_____
_____
_____
_____
_____

REFLECTIONS & THOUGHTS

_____
_____
_____
_____
_____
_____
_____
_____
_____
_____
_____
_____

PRAYER REQUEST

_____
_____
_____
_____
_____

DAY AND DATE _____ ___/___/____

"Let the morning bring me word of your unfailing love, for I have put my trust in you. Show me the way I should go, for to you I entrust my life."

Psalm 143:8

MY LORD, I AM THANKFUL FOR

_____
_____
_____
_____
_____

REFLECTIONS & THOUGHTS

_____
_____
_____
_____
_____
_____
_____
_____
_____
_____
_____

PRAYER REQUEST

_____
_____
_____
_____

DAY AND DATE _____ ___/___/____

Psalm 143:8

MY LORD, I AM THANKFUL FOR

REFLECTIONS & THOUGHTS

PRAYER REQUEST

"Honor your father and mother, and love your neighbor as yourself."

Matthew 19:19

MY LORD, I AM THANKFUL FOR

REFLECTIONS & THOUGHTS

PRAYER REQUEST

31 DAYS OF GOD'S LOVE

"Though the mountains be shaken and the hills be removed, yet my unfailing love for you will not be shaken nor my covenant of peace be removed," says the Lord, who has compassion on you."

Isaiah 54:10

All Scripture is a symphony of God's love for man. God offers man Paradise, gives him immortality, happiness and security. He creates man in his image and equips him with a rational soul, conscience and free will, which proves God's great love for man. He announces the coming His Son, as someone who has to buy out the human guilt - "For God so loved the world that He gave His one and only Son, that whoever believes in Him shall not perish but have eternal life." - John 3:16.

We should strive for the love that God has given us. He loved us with a true, full and completely unconditional love. In Jesus Christ, God's love is most fully revealed. He voluntarily accepted the unjust punishment and surrendered himself to the torturers for our salvation. Being aware of God's love so great, let us love one another. The only source of true love - capable of loving one's neighbor and even loving one's enemy, capable of forgiving and forgetting - is God himself, as Jesus testifies to us: "As the Father has loved me, so have I loved you. Now remain in my love." (John 15: 9).

MY THOUGHTS

DAY AND DATE _____ ___/___/_____

"This is love: not that we loved God, but that he loved us and sent his Son as an atoning sacrifice for our sins."

1 John 4:10

MY LORD, I AM THANKFUL FOR

REFLECTIONS & THOUGHTS

PRAYER REQUEST

"The Lord is compassionate and gracious, slow to anger, abounding in love."

Psalm 103:8

MY LORD, I AM THANKFUL FOR

_____
_____
_____
_____
_____

REFLECTIONS & THOUGHTS

_____
_____
_____
_____
_____
_____
_____
_____
_____
_____
_____

PRAYER REQUEST

_____
_____
_____
_____

" And walk in the way of love, just as Christ loved us and gave himself up for us as a fragrant offering and sacrifice to God."

Ephesians 5:2

MY LORD, I AM THANKFUL FOR

_____
_____
_____
_____
_____

REFLECTIONS & THOUGHTS

_____
_____
_____
_____
_____
_____
_____
_____
_____
_____
_____

PRAYER REQUEST

_____
_____
_____
_____
_____

"We love because He first loved us."

1 John 4:19

MY LORD, I AM THANKFUL FOR

_____
_____
_____
_____
_____

REFLECTIONS & THOUGHTS

_____
_____
_____
_____
_____
_____
_____
_____
_____
_____
_____
_____

PRAYER REQUEST

_____
_____
_____
_____

DAY AND DATE _____ ___/___/____

MY LORD, I AM THANKFUL FOR

REFLECTIONS & THOUGHTS

PRAYER REQUEST

DAY AND DATE _____ / / ___

MY LORD, I AM THANKFUL FOR

REFLECTIONS & THOUGHTS

PRAYER REQUEST

"See what great love the Father has lavished on us, that we should be called children of God! And that is what we are! The reason the world does not know us is that it did not know him."

1 John 3:1

MY LORD, I AM THANKFUL FOR

_____
_____
_____
_____

REFLECTIONS & THOUGHTS

_____
_____
_____
_____
_____
_____
_____
_____
_____
_____
_____
_____

PRAYER REQUEST

_____
_____
_____
_____

When I said, "My foot is slipping,"your unfailing love, Lord, supported me

Psalm 94:18

MY LORD, I AM THANKFUL FOR

_____

_____

_____

_____

_____

REFLECTIONS & THOUGHTS

_____

_____

_____

_____

_____

_____

_____

_____

_____

_____

_____

PRAYER REQUEST

_____

_____

_____

_____

DAY AND DATE _____ ___/___/_____

"Because Your love is better than life, my lips will glorify You. I will praise You as long as I live, and in Your name I will lift up my hands."

Psalm 63:3-4

MY LORD, I AM THANKFUL FOR

REFLECTIONS & THOUGHTS

PRAYER REQUEST

51

"No, in all these things we are more than conquerors through him who loved us."

Romans 8:37

MY LORD, I AM THANKFUL FOR

_____
_____
_____
_____
_____

REFLECTIONS & THOUGHTS

_____
_____
_____
_____
_____
_____
_____
_____
_____
_____
_____
_____

PRAYER REQUEST

_____
_____
_____
_____

DAY AND DATE _____ ___/___/_____

MY LORD, I AM THANKFUL FOR

_____

_____

_____

_____

_____

REFLECTIONS & THOUGHTS

_____

_____

_____

_____

_____

_____

_____

_____

_____

_____

_____

_____

_____

PRAYER REQUEST

_____

_____

_____

_____

DAY AND DATE _____ ___/___/_____

"No one has ever seen God; but if we love one another, God lives in us and his love is made complete in us."

1 John 4:12

MY LORD, I AM THANKFUL FOR

_____
_____
_____
_____
_____

REFLECTIONS & THOUGHTS

_____
_____
_____
_____
_____
_____
_____
_____
_____
_____
_____

PRAYER REQUEST

_____
_____
_____
_____
_____

"Have I not commanded you? Be strong and courageous. Do not be afraid; do not be discouraged, for the Lord your God will be with you wherever you go."

Joshua 1:9

MY LORD, I AM THANKFUL FOR

_____
_____
_____
_____
_____

REFLECTIONS & THOUGHTS

_____
_____
_____
_____
_____
_____
_____
_____
_____
_____
_____
_____

PRAYER REQUEST

_____
_____
_____
_____

DAY AND DATE _____ ___/___/_____

"I can do all this through him who gives me strength."

Philippians 4:13

MY LORD, I AM THANKFUL FOR

_____
_____
_____
_____
_____

REFLECTIONS & THOUGHTS

_____
_____
_____
_____
_____
_____
_____
_____
_____
_____
_____

PRAYER REQUEST

_____
_____
_____
_____

DAY AND DATE _____ ___/___/_____

"For every house is built by someone, but God is the builder of everything."

Hebrews 3:4

MY LORD, I AM THANKFUL FOR

_____

_____

_____

_____

REFLECTIONS & THOUGHTS

_____

_____

_____

_____

_____

_____

_____

_____

_____

_____

PRAYER REQUEST

_____

_____

_____

_____

"And so we know and rely on the love God has for us. God is love.
Whoever lives in love lives in God, and God in them. "

1 John 4:16

MY LORD, I AM THANKFUL FOR

_____
_____
_____
_____
_____

REFLECTIONS & THOUGHTS

_____
_____
_____
_____
_____
_____
_____
_____
_____
_____
_____

PRAYER REQUEST

_____
_____
_____
_____
_____

DAY AND DATE _____ ___/___/_____

"For those who find me find life and receive favor from the Lord. "

Proverbs 8:35

MY LORD, I AM THANKFUL FOR

_____
_____
_____
_____
_____

REFLECTIONS & THOUGHTS

_____
_____
_____
_____
_____
_____
_____
_____
_____
_____
_____
_____
_____

PRAYER REQUEST

_____
_____
_____
_____
_____

DAY AND DATE _____ ___/___/___

MY LORD, I AM THANKFUL FOR

_____
_____
_____
_____
_____

REFLECTIONS & THOUGHTS

_____
_____
_____
_____
_____
_____
_____
_____
_____
_____
_____

PRAYER REQUEST

_____
_____
_____
_____

DAY AND DATE _____ ___ / ___ / _____

"The grass withers and the flowers fall, but the word of our God endures forever."

Isaiah 40:8

MY LORD, I AM THANKFUL FOR

_____
_____
_____
_____
_____

REFLECTIONS & THOUGHTS

_____
_____
_____
_____
_____
_____
_____
_____
_____
_____
_____
_____

PRAYER REQUEST

_____
_____
_____
_____

"In the beginning was the Word, and the Word was with God, and the Word was God."

John 1:1

MY LORD, I AM THANKFUL FOR

_____
_____
_____
_____
_____

REFLECTIONS & THOUGHTS

_____
_____
_____
_____
_____
_____
_____
_____
_____
_____
_____
_____

PRAYER REQUEST

_____
_____
_____
_____
_____

DAY AND DATE _____ ___/___/_____

"This is the message we have heard from him and declare to you: God is light; in him there is no darkness at all."

1 John 1:5

MY LORD, I AM THANKFUL FOR

REFLECTIONS & THOUGHTS

PRAYER REQUEST

DAY AND DATE _____ ___ / ___ / _____

"Everyone who calls on the name of the Lord will be saved."

Romans 10:13

MY LORD, I AM THANKFUL FOR

_____
_____
_____
_____
_____

REFLECTIONS & THOUGHTS

_____
_____
_____
_____
_____
_____
_____
_____
_____
_____
_____
_____

PRAYER REQUEST

_____
_____
_____
_____

DAY AND DATE _____ ___/___/___

While he was still speaking, a bright cloud covered them, and a voice from the cloud said, "This is my Son, whom I love; with him I am well pleased. Listen to him!"

Matthew 17:5

MY LORD, I AM THANKFUL FOR

_____

_____

_____

_____

REFLECTIONS & THOUGHTS

_____

_____

_____

_____

_____

_____

_____

_____

_____

_____

_____

PRAYER REQUEST

_____

_____

_____

_____

"For I am the Lord your God who takes hold of your right hand and says to you, Do not fear; I will help you."

Isaiah 41:13

MY LORD, I AM THANKFUL FOR

_____
_____
_____
_____
_____

REFLECTIONS & THOUGHTS

_____
_____
_____
_____
_____
_____
_____
_____
_____
_____
_____
_____
_____

PRAYER REQUEST

_____
_____
_____
_____

"So God created mankind in his own image, in the image of God he created them; male and female he created them."

Genesis 1:27

MY LORD, I AM THANKFUL FOR

_____
_____
_____
_____
_____

REFLECTIONS & THOUGHTS

_____
_____
_____
_____
_____
_____
_____
_____
_____
_____
_____

PRAYER REQUEST

_____
_____
_____
_____

"May the grace of the Lord Jesus Christ, and the love of God, and the fellowship of the Holy Spirit be with you all."

2 Corinthians 13:14

MY LORD, I AM THANKFUL FOR

_____
_____
_____
_____
_____

REFLECTIONS & THOUGHTS

_____
_____
_____
_____
_____
_____
_____
_____
_____
_____
_____
_____

PRAYER REQUEST

_____
_____
_____
_____

DAY AND DATE _____ ___/___/_____

"But do not forget this one thing, dear friends: With the Lord a day is like a thousand years, and a thousand years are like a day."

2 Peter 3:8

MY LORD, I AM THANKFUL FOR

REFLECTIONS & THOUGHTS

PRAYER REQUEST

DAY AND DATE _____ ___/___/_____

MY LORD, I AM THANKFUL FOR

_____

_____

_____

_____

_____

REFLECTIONS & THOUGHTS

_____

_____

_____

_____

_____

_____

_____

_____

_____

_____

_____

PRAYER REQUEST

_____

_____

_____

_____

DAY AND DATE _____ ___/___/_____

"The Lord your God is in your midst — a warrior bringing victory. He will create calm with his love; he will rejoice over you with singing."

Zephaniah 3:17

MY LORD, I AM THANKFUL FOR

_____
_____
_____
_____
_____

REFLECTIONS & THOUGHTS

_____
_____
_____
_____
_____
_____
_____
_____
_____
_____
_____

PRAYER REQUEST

_____
_____
_____
_____

"Know now then that the Lord your God is the only true God! He is the faithful God, who keeps the covenant and proves loyal to everyone who loves him and keeps his commands — even to the thousandth generation!"

Deuteronomy 7:9

MY LORD, I AM THANKFUL FOR

_____
_____
_____
_____
_____
_____

REFLECTIONS & THOUGHTS

_____
_____
_____
_____
_____
_____
_____
_____
_____
_____
_____
_____
_____

PRAYER REQUEST

_____
_____
_____
_____

DAY AND DATE _____ ___/___/_____

"Give thanks to the Lord because he is good, because his faithful love endures forever."

1 Chronicles 16:34

MY LORD, I AM THANKFUL FOR

_____
_____
_____
_____
_____

REFLECTIONS & THOUGHTS

_____
_____
_____
_____
_____
_____
_____
_____
_____
_____
_____

PRAYER REQUEST

_____
_____
_____
_____

31 DAYS OF FORGIVENESS

Then Peter came to Jesus and asked, "Lord, how many times shall I forgive my brother or sister who sins against me? Up to seven times?" Jesus answered, "I tell you, not seven times, but seventy-seven times."

Matthew 18:21-22

It might seem that forgiveness would be easy if we had to forgive only those who come to us with repentance and sincerely regret what they have done to us. However, the point is to forgive unconditionally everyone. Holding a grudge against our neighbor in our hearts, we distance ourselves from God. Forgiveness is our own choice, we decide whether we want to come closer to God or still live in the past. So let's get rid of any resentments and let us turn to God - He knows what is best for us and will always show us the right path.

We have sinned against God far more than anyone has ever sinned against us. If God forgives us so much, how can we not forgive others for that little? God promises us that when we come to Him and ask for forgiveness, He will graciously grant it to us (1 John 1: 9). The forgiveness we give should have no limits, just as God's forgiveness for us is infinite (Luke 17: 3-4).

MY THOUGHTS

"Therefore let us stop passing judgment on one another. Instead, make up your mind not to put any stumbling block or obstacle in the way of a brother or sister."

Romans 14:13

MY LORD, I AM THANKFUL FOR

REFLECTIONS & THOUGHTS

PRAYER REQUEST

DAY AND DATE _____ ___/___/_____

MY LORD, I AM THANKFUL FOR

_____
_____
_____
_____
_____

REFLECTIONS & THOUGHTS

_____
_____
_____
_____
_____
_____
_____
_____
_____
_____
_____
_____

PRAYER REQUEST

_____
_____
_____
_____
_____

DAY AND DATE _____ ___/___/_____

"Hatred stirs up conflict, but love covers over all wrongs."

Proverbs 10:12

MY LORD, I AM THANKFUL FOR

_____
_____
_____
_____
_____

REFLECTIONS & THOUGHTS

_____
_____
_____
_____
_____
_____
_____
_____
_____
_____
_____
_____

PRAYER REQUEST

_____
_____
_____
_____

DAY AND DATE _____ __/__/____

"You intended to harm me, but God intended it for good to accomplish what is now being done, the saving of many lives."

Genesis 50:20

MY LORD, I AM THANKFUL FOR

_____
_____
_____
_____
_____

REFLECTIONS & THOUGHTS

_____
_____
_____
_____
_____
_____
_____
_____
_____
_____
_____
_____

PRAYER REQUEST

_____
_____
_____
_____

"Whoever would foster love covers over an offense, but whoever repeats the matter separates close friends."

Proverbs 17:9

MY LORD, I AM THANKFUL FOR

_____
_____
_____
_____
_____

REFLECTIONS & THOUGHTS

_____
_____
_____
_____
_____
_____
_____
_____
_____
_____
_____
_____

PRAYER REQUEST

_____
_____
_____
_____
_____

DAY AND DATE _____ __/__/____

MY LORD, I AM THANKFUL FOR

_____
_____
_____
_____
_____

REFLECTIONS & THOUGHTS

_____
_____
_____
_____
_____
_____
_____
_____
_____
_____
_____

PRAYER REQUEST

_____
_____
_____
_____

"For if you forgive other people when they sin against you, your heavenly Father will also forgive you."

Matthew 6:14

MY LORD, I AM THANKFUL FOR

_____
_____
_____
_____
_____

REFLECTIONS & THOUGHTS

_____
_____
_____
_____
_____
_____
_____
_____
_____
_____
_____
_____

PRAYER REQUEST

_____
_____
_____
_____

DAY AND DATE _____ ___ / ___ / ___

"Do not judge, and you will not be judged. Do not condemn, and you will not be condemned. Forgive, and you will be forgiven."

Luke 6:37

MY LORD, I AM THANKFUL FOR

_____

_____

_____

_____

REFLECTIONS & THOUGHTS

_____

_____

_____

_____

_____

_____

_____

_____

_____

_____

PRAYER REQUEST

_____

_____

_____

_____

"And when you stand praying, if you hold anything against anyone, forgive them, so that your Father in heaven may forgive you your sins."

Mark 11:25

MY LORD, I AM THANKFUL FOR

_____
_____
_____
_____
_____

REFLECTIONS & THOUGHTS

_____
_____
_____
_____
_____
_____
_____
_____
_____
_____
_____
_____

PRAYER REQUEST

_____
_____
_____
_____

DAY AND DATE _____ /___/_____

"For the Lord your God is gracious and compassionate. He will not turn His face from you if you return to Him."

2 Chronicles 30:9b

MY LORD, I AM THANKFUL FOR

_____
_____
_____
_____
_____

REFLECTIONS & THOUGHTS

_____
_____
_____
_____
_____
_____
_____
_____
_____
_____
_____
_____

PRAYER REQUEST

_____
_____
_____
_____

DAY AND DATE _____ ___/___/_____

MY LORD, I AM THANKFUL FOR

_____
_____
_____
_____
_____

REFLECTIONS & THOUGHTS

_____
_____
_____
_____
_____
_____
_____
_____
_____
_____
_____
_____

PRAYER REQUEST

_____
_____
_____
_____
_____

DAY AND DATE _____ ___/___/_____

"And forgive us our debts, as we also have forgiven our debtors."

Matthew 6:12

MY LORD, I AM THANKFUL FOR

_____

_____

_____

_____

_____

REFLECTIONS & THOUGHTS

_____

_____

_____

_____

_____

_____

_____

_____

_____

_____

_____

_____

PRAYER REQUEST

_____

_____

_____

_____

"But in your great mercy you did not put an end to them or abandon them, for you are a gracious and merciful God."

Nehemiah 9:31

MY LORD, I AM THANKFUL FOR

REFLECTIONS & THOUGHTS

PRAYER REQUEST

"If your brother or sister sins against you, rebuke them; and if they repent, forgive them. Even if they sin against you seven times in a day and seven times come back to you saying 'I repent,' you must forgive them."

Luke 17:3b-4

MY LORD, I AM THANKFUL FOR

REFLECTIONS & THOUGHTS

PRAYER REQUEST

"For I will forgive their wickedness and will remember their sins no more."

Hebrews 8:12

MY LORD, I AM THANKFUL FOR

_____
_____
_____
_____
_____

REFLECTIONS & THOUGHTS

_____
_____
_____
_____
_____
_____
_____
_____
_____
_____
_____

PRAYER REQUEST

_____
_____
_____
_____

DAY AND DATE _____ ____/____/____

MY LORD, I AM THANKFUL FOR

REFLECTIONS & THOUGHTS

PRAYER REQUEST

DAY AND DATE _____ __ / __ / ____

"And so I tell you, every kind of sin and slander can be forgiven, but blasphemy against the Spirit will not be forgiven."

Matthew 12:31

MY LORD, I AM THANKFUL FOR

REFLECTIONS & THOUGHTS

PRAYER REQUEST

DAY AND DATE _____ __/__/____

"Blessed is the one whose transgressions are forgiven, whose sins are covered."

Psalm 32:1

MY LORD, I AM THANKFUL FOR

_____
_____
_____
_____
_____

REFLECTIONS & THOUGHTS

_____
_____
_____
_____
_____
_____
_____
_____
_____
_____
_____
_____

PRAYER REQUEST

_____
_____
_____
_____

DAY AND DATE _____ ___/___/_____

"Peter replied, "Repent and be baptized, every one of you, in the name of Jesus Christ for the forgiveness of your sins. And you will receive the gift of the Holy Spirit."

Acts 2:38

MY LORD, I AM THANKFUL FOR

_____

_____

_____

_____

_____

REFLECTIONS & THOUGHTS

_____

_____

_____

_____

_____

_____

_____

_____

_____

_____

_____

_____

PRAYER REQUEST

_____

_____

_____

_____

"Let the wicked forsake their ways and the unrighteous their thoughts.
Let them turn to the Lord, and he will have mercy on them, and to our
God, for he will freely pardon."

Isaiah 55:7

MY LORD, I AM THANKFUL FOR

_____
_____
_____
_____

REFLECTIONS & THOUGHTS

_____
_____
_____
_____
_____
_____
_____
_____
_____
_____
_____

PRAYER REQUEST

_____
_____
_____
_____

"Repent, then, and turn to God, so that your sins may be wiped out, that times of refreshing may come from the Lord."

Acts 3:19

MY LORD, I AM THANKFUL FOR

_____
_____
_____
_____
_____

REFLECTIONS & THOUGHTS

_____
_____
_____
_____
_____
_____
_____
_____
_____
_____
_____

PRAYER REQUEST

_____
_____
_____
_____

"For sin shall no longer be your master, because you are not under the law, but under grace."

Romans 6:14

MY LORD, I AM THANKFUL FOR

_____
_____
_____
_____

REFLECTIONS & THOUGHTS

_____
_____
_____
_____
_____
_____
_____
_____
_____
_____
_____
_____

PRAYER REQUEST

_____
_____
_____
_____

"The grace of the Lord Jesus Christ be with your spirit."

Philemon 1:25

MY LORD, I AM THANKFUL FOR

_____
_____
_____
_____
_____

REFLECTIONS & THOUGHTS

_____
_____
_____
_____
_____
_____
_____
_____
_____
_____
_____
_____
_____

PRAYER REQUEST

_____
_____
_____
_____
_____

DAY AND DATE _____ ___/___/___

"Surely your goodness and love will follow me all the days of my life,
and I will dwell in the house of the Lord forever."

Psalm 23:6

MY LORD, I AM THANKFUL FOR

_____
_____
_____
_____
_____

REFLECTIONS & THOUGHTS

_____
_____
_____
_____
_____
_____
_____
_____
_____
_____
_____
_____

PRAYER REQUEST

_____
_____
_____
_____

"So that, just as sin reigned in death, so also grace might reign through righteousness to bring eternal life through Jesus Christ our Lord."

Romans 5:21

MY LORD, I AM THANKFUL FOR

_____
_____
_____
_____
_____

REFLECTIONS & THOUGHTS

_____
_____
_____
_____
_____
_____
_____
_____
_____
_____
_____
_____

PRAYER REQUEST

_____
_____
_____
_____

"Whoever conceals their sins does not prosper, but the one who confesses and renounces them finds mercy."

Proverbs 28:13

MY LORD, I AM THANKFUL FOR

_____

_____

_____

_____

REFLECTIONS & THOUGHTS

_____

_____

_____

_____

_____

_____

_____

_____

_____

_____

_____

PRAYER REQUEST

_____

_____

_____

_____

DAY AND DATE _____ ___/___/_____

"Do not withhold your mercy from me, Lord; may your love and
faithfulness always protect me."

Psalm 40:11

MY LORD, I AM THANKFUL FOR

_____
_____
_____
_____
_____

REFLECTIONS & THOUGHTS

_____
_____
_____
_____
_____
_____
_____
_____
_____
_____
_____

PRAYER REQUEST

_____
_____
_____
_____

"Good will come to those who are generous and lend freely, who conduct their affairs with justice."

Psalm 112:5

MY LORD, I AM THANKFUL FOR

_____
_____
_____
_____
_____

REFLECTIONS & THOUGHTS

_____
_____
_____
_____
_____
_____
_____
_____
_____
_____
_____

PRAYER REQUEST

_____
_____
_____
_____

"For it has been granted to you on behalf of Christ not only to believe in him, but also to suffer for him."

Philippians 1:29

MY LORD, I AM THANKFUL FOR

_____
_____
_____
_____
_____

REFLECTIONS & THOUGHTS

_____
_____
_____
_____
_____
_____
_____
_____
_____
_____
_____

PRAYER REQUEST

_____
_____
_____
_____

DAY AND DATE _____ ___/___/_____

MY LORD, I AM THANKFUL FOR

_____

_____

_____

_____

_____

REFLECTIONS & THOUGHTS

_____

_____

_____

_____

_____

_____

_____

_____

_____

_____

_____

PRAYER REQUEST

_____

_____

_____

_____

DAY AND DATE _____ ____/____/_____

MY LORD, I AM THANKFUL FOR

REFLECTIONS & THOUGHTS

PRAYER REQUEST

31 DAYS OF FAITH AND HOPE

"Why, my soul, are you downcast?
Why so disturbed within me?
Put your hope in God,
for I will yet praise him,
my Savior and my God."

Psalm 42:11

As we begin to study the Bible from the first pages of it, we will find that all God's promises are fulfilled in the course of time as foretold. The Bible says: "Know also that wisdom is like honey for you: If you find it, there is a future hope for you, and your hope will not be cut off." (Proverbs 24:14). There are many examples of faith and hope in the Old Testament. The man in all circumstances of his life is simply to trust God and surrender to His judgments. A perfect example of such an attitude is the behavior of Hiob. He lost everything, but his faith and hope were steadfast. God rewarded his suffering and returned everything to him.

As for the New Testament, hope finds its fulfillment in the person and actions of Jesus of Nazareth. This applies above all to his glorious resurrection and our certainty in faith that the Son of God will never leave us alone, not only here on this earth (*"I am with you all the days, until the end of the world"* - Mt 28:20), but also in eternity by offering us salvation. We must believe and hope to the end, no matter what.

MY THOUGHTS

DAY AND DATE _____ ___/___/_____

"Whoever dwells in the shelter of the Most High will rest in the shadow of the Almighty. I will say of the Lord, "He is my refuge and my fortress, my God, in whom I trust."

Psalm 91:1-2

MY LORD, I AM THANKFUL FOR

_____
_____
_____
_____
_____

REFLECTIONS & THOUGHTS

_____
_____
_____
_____
_____
_____
_____
_____
_____
_____
_____

PRAYER REQUEST

_____
_____
_____
_____

"This is the confidence we have in approaching God: that if we ask
anything according to his will, he hears us."

1 John 5:14

MY LORD, I AM THANKFUL FOR

_____
_____
_____
_____
_____

REFLECTIONS & THOUGHTS

_____
_____
_____
_____
_____
_____
_____
_____
_____
_____
_____
_____
_____

PRAYER REQUEST

_____
_____
_____
_____

DAY AND DATE _____ ___/___/_____

"For I know the plans I have for you, declares the Lord, plans to prosper you and not to harm you, plans to give you hope and a future."

Jeremiah 29:11

MY LORD, I AM THANKFUL FOR

REFLECTIONS & THOUGHTS

PRAYER REQUEST

DAY AND DATE _____ ___/___/____

MY LORD, I AM THANKFUL FOR

_____
_____
_____
_____
_____

REFLECTIONS & THOUGHTS

_____
_____
_____
_____
_____
_____
_____
_____
_____
_____
_____
_____

PRAYER REQUEST

_____
_____
_____
_____

DAY AND DATE _____ ___/___/_____

"Come to me, all you who are weary and burdened, and I will give you rest."

Matthew 11:28

MY LORD, I AM THANKFUL FOR

_____
_____
_____
_____
_____

REFLECTIONS & THOUGHTS

_____
_____
_____
_____
_____
_____
_____
_____
_____
_____
_____

PRAYER REQUEST

_____
_____
_____
_____

DAY AND DATE _____ ___ / ___ / _____

"The Lord is near to all who call on him, to all who call on him in truth."

Psalm 145:18

MY LORD, I AM THANKFUL FOR

_____

_____

_____

_____

_____

REFLECTIONS & THOUGHTS

_____

_____

_____

_____

_____

_____

_____

_____

_____

_____

_____

_____

PRAYER REQUEST

_____

_____

_____

_____

DAY AND DATE _____ ___/___/_____

"But as for me, I watch in hope for the Lord, I wait for God my Savior;
my God will hear me."

Micah 7:7

MY LORD, I AM THANKFUL FOR

_____
_____
_____
_____
_____

REFLECTIONS & THOUGHTS

_____
_____
_____
_____
_____
_____
_____
_____
_____
_____
_____

PRAYER REQUEST

_____
_____
_____
_____

DAY AND DATE _____ ___/___/_____

So we say with confidence, "The Lord is my helper; I will not be afraid.
What can mere mortals do to me?"

Hebrews 13:6

MY LORD, I AM THANKFUL FOR

_____
_____
_____
_____

REFLECTIONS & THOUGHTS

_____
_____
_____
_____
_____
_____
_____
_____
_____
_____

PRAYER REQUEST

_____
_____
_____
_____

DAY AND DATE _____ ___/___/_____

"You are my refuge and my shield; I have put my hope in your word."

Psalm 119:114

MY LORD, I AM THANKFUL FOR

_____
_____
_____
_____
_____

REFLECTIONS & THOUGHTS

_____
_____
_____
_____
_____
_____
_____
_____
_____
_____
_____

PRAYER REQUEST

_____
_____
_____
_____

DAY AND DATE _____ ___/___/___

MY LORD, I AM THANKFUL FOR

_____
_____
_____
_____
_____

REFLECTIONS & THOUGHTS

_____
_____
_____
_____
_____
_____
_____
_____
_____
_____
_____
_____
_____

PRAYER REQUEST

_____
_____
_____
_____

DAY AND DATE _____ __/__/____

MY LORD, I AM THANKFUL FOR

_____
_____
_____
_____
_____

REFLECTIONS & THOUGHTS

_____
_____
_____
_____
_____
_____
_____
_____
_____
_____
_____

PRAYER REQUEST

_____
_____
_____
_____

"For physical training is of some value, but godliness has value for all things, holding promise for both the present life and the life to come."

1 Timothy 4:8

MY LORD, I AM THANKFUL FOR

_____
_____
_____
_____
_____

REFLECTIONS & THOUGHTS

_____
_____
_____
_____
_____
_____
_____
_____
_____
_____
_____
_____

PRAYER REQUEST

_____
_____
_____
_____
_____

DAY AND DATE _____ ___/___/____

"Therefore I tell you, whatever you ask for in prayer, believe that you have received it, and it will be yours."

Mark 11:24

MY LORD, I AM THANKFUL FOR

_____
_____
_____
_____
_____

REFLECTIONS & THOUGHTS

_____
_____
_____
_____
_____
_____
_____
_____
_____
_____
_____

PRAYER REQUEST

_____
_____
_____
_____

DAY AND DATE _____ ___/___/____

"Now faith is confidence in what we hope for and assurance about what we do not see."

Hebrews 11:1

MY LORD, I AM THANKFUL FOR

_____
_____
_____
_____
_____

REFLECTIONS & THOUGHTS

_____
_____
_____
_____
_____
_____
_____
_____
_____
_____
_____
_____

PRAYER REQUEST

_____
_____
_____
_____

DAY AND DATE _____ __/__/____

"But when you ask, you must believe and not doubt, because the one who doubts is like a wave of the sea, blown and tossed by the wind."

James 1:6

MY LORD, I AM THANKFUL FOR

_____
_____
_____
_____
_____

REFLECTIONS & THOUGHTS

_____
_____
_____
_____
_____
_____
_____
_____
_____
_____
_____

PRAYER REQUEST

_____
_____
_____
_____

DAY AND DATE _____ ___/___/_____

"If you can?" said Jesus. "Everything is possible for one who believes."

Mark 9:23

MY LORD, I AM THANKFUL FOR

_____
_____
_____
_____
_____

REFLECTIONS & THOUGHTS

_____
_____
_____
_____
_____
_____
_____
_____
_____
_____
_____

PRAYER REQUEST

_____
_____
_____
_____

DAY AND DATE _____ ___/___/____

Jesus said to her, "I am the resurrection and the life. The one who
believes in me will live, even though they die; and whoever lives by
believing in me will never die. Do you believe this?"

John 11:25-26

MY LORD, I AM THANKFUL FOR

REFLECTIONS & THOUGHTS

PRAYER REQUEST

"And by faith even Sarah, who was past childbearing age, was enabled to bear children because she considered him faithful who had made the promise."

Hebrews 11:11

MY LORD, I AM THANKFUL FOR

_____
_____
_____
_____
_____

REFLECTIONS & THOUGHTS

_____
_____
_____
_____
_____
_____
_____
_____
_____
_____
_____
_____

PRAYER REQUEST

_____
_____
_____
_____

DAY AND DATE _____ ___/___/___

Then Jesus declared, "I am the bread of life. Whoever comes to me will never go hungry, and whoever believes in me will never be thirsty."

John 6:35

MY LORD, I AM THANKFUL FOR

_____
_____
_____
_____
_____

REFLECTIONS & THOUGHTS

_____
_____
_____
_____
_____
_____
_____
_____
_____
_____
_____

PRAYER REQUEST

_____
_____
_____
_____

"Go," said Jesus, "your faith has healed you." Immediately he received his sight and followed Jesus along the road.

Mark 10:52

MY LORD, I AM THANKFUL FOR

_____
_____
_____
_____

REFLECTIONS & THOUGHTS

_____
_____
_____
_____
_____
_____
_____
_____
_____
_____

PRAYER REQUEST

_____
_____
_____
_____

DAY AND DATE _____ ___/___/___

"Be on your guard; stand firm in the faith; be courageous; be strong."

1 Corinthians 16:13

MY LORD, I AM THANKFUL FOR

_____
_____
_____
_____
_____

REFLECTIONS & THOUGHTS

_____
_____
_____
_____
_____
_____
_____
_____
_____
_____
_____

PRAYER REQUEST

_____
_____
_____
_____

DAY AND DATE _____ ___/___/_____

"So in Christ Jesus you are all children of God through faith, for all of you who were baptized into Christ have clothed yourselves with Christ."

Galatians 3:26-27

MY LORD, I AM THANKFUL FOR

REFLECTIONS & THOUGHTS

PRAYER REQUEST

DAY AND DATE _____ ___/___/____

But the angel said to them, "Do not be afraid. I bring you good news
that will cause great joy for all the people."

Luke 2:10

MY LORD, I AM THANKFUL FOR

_____
_____
_____
_____
_____

REFLECTIONS & THOUGHTS

_____
_____
_____
_____
_____
_____
_____
_____
_____
_____
_____

PRAYER REQUEST

_____
_____
_____
_____

DAY AND DATE _____ ___/___/____

MY LORD, I AM THANKFUL FOR

_____
_____
_____
_____
_____

REFLECTIONS & THOUGHTS

_____
_____
_____
_____
_____
_____
_____
_____
_____
_____
_____
_____

PRAYER REQUEST

_____
_____
_____
_____
_____

DAY AND DATE _____ ___/___/_____

"Fixing our eyes on Jesus, the pioneer and perfecter of faith. For the joy set before him he endured the cross, scorning its shame, and sat down at the right hand of the throne of God."

Hebrews 12:2

MY LORD, I AM THANKFUL FOR

_____
_____
_____
_____
_____

REFLECTIONS & THOUGHTS

_____
_____
_____
_____
_____
_____
_____
_____
_____
_____
_____
_____

PRAYER REQUEST

_____
_____
_____
_____
_____

"Whoever believes in me, as Scripture has said, rivers of living water will flow from within them."

John 7:38

MY LORD, I AM THANKFUL FOR

_____
_____
_____
_____
_____

REFLECTIONS & THOUGHTS

_____
_____
_____
_____
_____
_____
_____
_____
_____
_____
_____
_____
_____

PRAYER REQUEST

_____
_____
_____
_____

"Truly I tell you, if anyone says to this mountain, 'Go, throw yourself into the sea,' and does not doubt in their heart but believes that what they say will happen, it will be done for them."

Mark 11:23

MY LORD, I AM THANKFUL FOR

_____
_____
_____
_____
_____

REFLECTIONS & THOUGHTS

_____
_____
_____
_____
_____
_____
_____
_____
_____
_____
_____

PRAYER REQUEST

_____
_____
_____
_____
_____

"I have been crucified with Christ and I no longer live, but Christ lives in me. The life I now live in the body, I live by faith in the Son of God, who loved me and gave himself for me."

Galatians 2:20

MY LORD, I AM THANKFUL FOR

_____
_____
_____
_____
_____

REFLECTIONS & THOUGHTS

_____
_____
_____
_____
_____
_____
_____
_____
_____
_____
_____
_____

PRAYER REQUEST

_____
_____
_____
_____
_____

DAY AND DATE _____ __/__/____

MY LORD, I AM THANKFUL FOR

REFLECTIONS & THOUGHTS

PRAYER REQUEST

DAY AND DATE _____ ___/___/____

MY LORD, I AM THANKFUL FOR

_____

_____

_____

_____

_____

REFLECTIONS & THOUGHTS

_____

_____

_____

_____

_____

_____

_____

_____

_____

_____

_____

_____

PRAYER REQUEST

_____

_____

_____

_____

_____

DAY AND DATE _____ ___/___/_____

"Very truly I tell you, whoever believes in me will do the works I have been doing, and they will do even greater things than these, because I am going to the Father."

John 14:12

MY LORD, I AM THANKFUL FOR

_____
_____
_____
_____
_____

REFLECTIONS & THOUGHTS

_____
_____
_____
_____
_____
_____
_____
_____
_____
_____
_____

PRAYER REQUEST

_____
_____
_____
_____

31 DAYS OF HEALING

HOW TO SURVIVE IN THE TOUGHEST TIMES?

"Whoever does not take up their cross and follow me is not worthy of me."

Matthew 10:38

Everyone in their life experiences suffering sooner or later, it is an indispensable element of our life. Well, it is a time of testing faith and love. With God, we are able to survive anything, we just need to trust Him and He will guide us.

It is difficult to be happy in the face of suffering, yet the Bible says: " Consider it pure joy, my brothers and sisters, whenever you face trials of many kinds, because you know that the testing of your faith produces perseverance. Let perseverance finish its work so that you may be mature and complete, not lacking anything." James 1:2-4. We must be able to accept everything. These are the moments that teach us the most.

The Bible says: "It is unthinkable that God would do wrong, that the Almighty would pervert justice." (Hiob 34:12) one cannot therefore ask, "Why do the innocent suffer?" We suffer because suffering is part of our mortal life. It perfects us: " Blows and wounds scrub away evil, and beatings purge the inmost being." Proverbs 20:30 and is a test for us: " We are hard pressed on every side, but not crushed; perplexed, but not in despair; persecuted, but not abandoned; struck down, but not destroyed.

We always carry around in our body the death of Jesus, so that the life of Jesus may also be revealed in our body." 2 Corinthians 4:8-10
So if you are in some difficult moment in your life right now - don't give up. When you place your trust in God, He will always help you to go through your trials in your life and through them He will do something great in you.

MY THOUGHTS

DAY AND DATE _____ ___/___/___

MY LORD, I AM THANKFUL FOR

_____

_____

_____

_____

_____

REFLECTIONS & THOUGHTS

_____

_____

_____

_____

_____

_____

_____

_____

_____

_____

_____

PRAYER REQUEST

_____

_____

_____

_____

142

DAY AND DATE _____ ___/___/____

On hearing this, Jesus said, "It is not the healthy who need a doctor, but the sick."

Matthew 9:12

MY LORD, I AM THANKFUL FOR

_____
_____
_____
_____
_____

REFLECTIONS & THOUGHTS

_____
_____
_____
_____
_____
_____
_____
_____
_____
_____
_____

PRAYER REQUEST

_____
_____
_____
_____

DAY AND DATE _____ ___/___/_____

MY LORD, I AM THANKFUL FOR

_____
_____
_____
_____
_____

REFLECTIONS & THOUGHTS

_____
_____
_____
_____
_____
_____
_____
_____
_____
_____
_____
_____

PRAYER REQUEST

_____
_____
_____
_____
_____

"The Lord himself goes before you and will be with you; he will never leave you nor forsake you. Do not be afraid; do not be discouraged."

Deuteronomy 31:8

MY LORD, I AM THANKFUL FOR

REFLECTIONS & THOUGHTS

PRAYER REQUEST

DAY AND DATE _____ ___/___/_____

"Blessed are those who mourn, for they will be comforted."

Matthew 5:4

MY LORD, I AM THANKFUL FOR

_____
_____
_____
_____
_____

REFLECTIONS & THOUGHTS

_____
_____
_____
_____
_____
_____
_____
_____
_____
_____
_____
_____

PRAYER REQUEST

_____
_____
_____
_____

DAY AND DATE _____ ___/___/_____

"Cast all your anxiety on him because he cares for you."

1 Peter 5:7

MY LORD, I AM THANKFUL FOR

_____
_____
_____
_____
_____

REFLECTIONS & THOUGHTS

_____
_____
_____
_____
_____
_____
_____
_____
_____
_____
_____

PRAYER REQUEST

_____
_____
_____
_____

"For his anger lasts only a moment, but his favor lasts a lifetime; weeping may stay for the night, but rejoicing comes in the morning."

Psalm 30:5

MY LORD, I AM THANKFUL FOR

_____
_____
_____
_____
_____

REFLECTIONS & THOUGHTS

_____
_____
_____
_____
_____
_____
_____
_____
_____
_____
_____
_____

PRAYER REQUEST

_____
_____
_____
_____

"Sorrowful, yet always rejoicing; poor, yet making many rich; having nothing, and yet possessing everything."

2 Corinthians 6:10

MY LORD, I AM THANKFUL FOR

_____
_____
_____
_____
_____

REFLECTIONS & THOUGHTS

_____
_____
_____
_____
_____
_____
_____
_____
_____
_____
_____

PRAYER REQUEST

_____
_____
_____
_____

DAY AND DATE _____ ___/___/____

"Worship the Lord your God, and his blessing will be on your food and water. I will take away sickness from among you."

Exodus 23:25

MY LORD, I AM THANKFUL FOR

REFLECTIONS & THOUGHTS

PRAYER REQUEST

DAY AND DATE _____ ___/___/____

MY LORD, I AM THANKFUL FOR

_____
_____
_____
_____
_____

REFLECTIONS & THOUGHTS

_____
_____
_____
_____
_____
_____
_____
_____
_____
_____
_____

PRAYER REQUEST

_____
_____
_____
_____

"Not only so, but we also glory in our sufferings, because we know that suffering produces perseverance; perseverance, character; and character, hope."

Romans 5:3-4

MY LORD, I AM THANKFUL FOR

REFLECTIONS & THOUGHTS

PRAYER REQUEST

"For our light and momentary troubles are achieving for us an eternal glory that far outweighs them all."

2 Corinthians 4:17

MY LORD, I AM THANKFUL FOR

_____
_____
_____
_____
_____

REFLECTIONS & THOUGHTS

_____
_____
_____
_____
_____
_____
_____
_____
_____
_____
_____

PRAYER REQUEST

_____
_____
_____
_____

"Whoever finds their life will lose it, and whoever loses their life for my sake will find it."

Matthew 10:39

MY LORD, I AM THANKFUL FOR

_____
_____
_____
_____
_____

REFLECTIONS & THOUGHTS

_____
_____
_____
_____
_____
_____
_____
_____
_____
_____
_____
_____

PRAYER REQUEST

_____
_____
_____
_____

DAY AND DATE _____ ___/___/___

"So do not fear, for I am with you; do not be dismayed, for I am your God. I will strengthen you and help you; I will uphold you with my righteous right hand."

Isaiah 41:10

MY LORD, I AM THANKFUL FOR

_____
_____
_____
_____
_____

REFLECTIONS & THOUGHTS

_____
_____
_____
_____
_____
_____
_____
_____
_____
_____
_____
_____

PRAYER REQUEST

_____
_____
_____
_____
_____

"That is why, for Christ's sake, I delight in weaknesses, in insults, in hardships, in persecutions, in difficulties. For when I am weak, then I am strong."

2 Corinthians 12:10

MY LORD, I AM THANKFUL FOR

_____
_____
_____
_____
_____

REFLECTIONS & THOUGHTS

_____
_____
_____
_____
_____
_____
_____
_____
_____
_____
_____
_____

PRAYER REQUEST

_____
_____
_____
_____

DAY AND DATE _____ ___ / ___ / ____

"I consider that our present sufferings are not worth comparing with the glory that will be revealed in us."

Romans 8:18

MY LORD, I AM THANKFUL FOR

REFLECTIONS & THOUGHTS

PRAYER REQUEST

"I, even I, am he who comforts you. Who are you that you fear mere mortals, human beings who are but grass."

Isaiah 51:12

MY LORD, I AM THANKFUL FOR

_____
_____
_____
_____
_____

REFLECTIONS & THOUGHTS

_____
_____
_____
_____
_____
_____
_____
_____
_____
_____
_____
_____

PRAYER REQUEST

_____
_____
_____
_____

DAY AND DATE _____ ___/___/_____

MY LORD, I AM THANKFUL FOR

REFLECTIONS & THOUGHTS

PRAYER REQUEST

DAY AND DATE _____ ___/___/____

MY LORD, I AM THANKFUL FOR

_____

_____

_____

_____

REFLECTIONS & THOUGHTS

_____

_____

_____

_____

_____

_____

_____

_____

_____

_____

_____

PRAYER REQUEST

_____

_____

_____

_____

DAY AND DATE _____ ___/___/____

"Do not worry about your life, what you will eat; or about your body, what you will wear. For life is more than food, and the body more than clothes."

Luke 12:22b-23

MY LORD, I AM THANKFUL FOR

_____
_____
_____
_____
_____

REFLECTIONS & THOUGHTS

_____
_____
_____
_____
_____
_____
_____
_____
_____
_____
_____

PRAYER REQUEST

_____
_____
_____
_____
_____

161

DAY AND DATE _____ ___/___/____

"Therefore do not worry about tomorrow, for tomorrow will worry about itself. Each day has enough trouble of its own."

Matthew 6:34

MY LORD, I AM THANKFUL FOR

_____
_____
_____
_____
_____

REFLECTIONS & THOUGHTS

_____
_____
_____
_____
_____
_____
_____
_____
_____
_____
_____
_____

PRAYER REQUEST

_____
_____
_____
_____

DAY AND DATE _____ ___/___/_____

"Anxiety weighs down the heart, but a kind word cheers it up."

Proverbs 12:25

MY LORD, I AM THANKFUL FOR

REFLECTIONS & THOUGHTS

PRAYER REQUEST

DAY AND DATE _____ ___/___/____

MY LORD, I AM THANKFUL FOR

_____
_____
_____
_____
_____

REFLECTIONS & THOUGHTS

_____
_____
_____
_____
_____
_____
_____
_____
_____
_____
_____
_____
_____

PRAYER REQUEST

_____
_____
_____
_____
_____

DAY AND DATE _____ ___/___/____

"Consider the ravens: They do not sow or reap, they have no storeroom or barn; yet God feeds them. And how much more valuable you are than birds!"

Luke 12:24

MY LORD, I AM THANKFUL FOR

REFLECTIONS & THOUGHTS

PRAYER REQUEST

"You are the salt of the earth. But if the salt loses its saltiness, how can it be made salty again? It is no longer good for anything, except to be thrown out and trampled underfoot."

Matthew 5:13

MY LORD, I AM THANKFUL FOR

_____
_____
_____
_____
_____

REFLECTIONS & THOUGHTS

_____
_____
_____
_____
_____
_____
_____
_____
_____
_____
_____
_____

PRAYER REQUEST

_____
_____
_____
_____

DAY AND DATE _____ ___/___/_____

"Many will be purified, made spotless and refined, but the wicked will
continue to be wicked. None of the wicked will understand, but those who
are wise will understand."

Daniel 12:10

MY LORD, I AM THANKFUL FOR

_____
_____
_____
_____
_____

REFLECTIONS & THOUGHTS

_____
_____
_____
_____
_____
_____
_____
_____
_____
_____
_____
_____

PRAYER REQUEST

_____
_____
_____
_____

"Brothers and sisters, if someone is caught in a sin, you who live by the Spirit should restore that person gently. But watch yourselves, or you also may be tempted."

Galatians 6:1

MY LORD, I AM THANKFUL FOR

_____
_____
_____
_____
_____

REFLECTIONS & THOUGHTS

_____
_____
_____
_____
_____
_____
_____
_____
_____
_____
_____
_____

PRAYER REQUEST

_____
_____
_____
_____

DAY AND DATE _____ ___/___/____

"If this is so, then the Lord knows how to rescue the godly from trials and to hold the unrighteous for punishment on the day of judgment."

2 Peter 2:9

MY LORD, I AM THANKFUL FOR

_____
_____
_____
_____
_____

REFLECTIONS & THOUGHTS

_____
_____
_____
_____
_____
_____
_____
_____
_____
_____
_____

PRAYER REQUEST

_____
_____
_____
_____

DAY AND DATE _____ ___/___/____

"Can a mother forget the baby at her breast and have no compassion on the child she has borne? Though she may forget, I will not forget you! See, I have engraved you on the palms of my hands; your walls are ever before me. "

Isaiah 49:15-16

MY LORD, I AM THANKFUL FOR

_____
_____
_____
_____
_____

REFLECTIONS & THOUGHTS

_____
_____
_____
_____
_____
_____
_____
_____
_____
_____
_____
_____

PRAYER REQUEST

_____
_____
_____
_____

DAY AND DATE _____ ___/___/___

MY LORD, I AM THANKFUL FOR

_____
_____
_____
_____
_____

REFLECTIONS & THOUGHTS

_____
_____
_____
_____
_____
_____
_____
_____
_____
_____
_____

PRAYER REQUEST

_____
_____
_____
_____
_____

171

DAY AND DATE _____ ___/___/_____

"When anyone becomes aware that they are guilty in any of these matters,
they must confess in what way they have sinned."

Leviticus 5:5

MY LORD, I AM THANKFUL FOR

REFLECTIONS & THOUGHTS

PRAYER REQUEST

31 DAYS OF GENTLENESS AND PATIENCE

Saint Thomas Aquinas teaches us that gentleness is a moral virtue that relates to affection, because it enables us to control the anger that grows within us. A person who is angry with another usually wants revenge, but gentleness keeps us from this urge to retaliate, and therefore we can say that gentleness is the fruit of love.

Consider the conversation between Jesus and the Samaritan woman it is a perfect example of Jesus' gentleness. He didn't ruthlessly rebuke this woman for her sin and immorality in her life, which he had every reason to do under the law of the time. Rather, he told the woman the truth about her life with remarkable gentleness. With this attitude He won the Samaritan woman, which caused her to bring many people to Christ: "Come, see a man who told me everything I ever did. Could this be the Messiah?" ? (John 4:29). Gentleness is a wonderful character trait that is worth working on throughout our lives.

It's a sign of wisdom and the ability to remain calm. If the next time someone harms us or something happens against our will, let us maintain that inner peace. During these 31 days, calm down and find gentleness and patience in yourself.

MY THOUGHTS

DAY AND DATE _____ ___/___/___

MY LORD, I AM THANKFUL FOR

_____
_____
_____
_____
_____

REFLECTIONS & THOUGHTS

_____
_____
_____
_____
_____
_____
_____
_____
_____
_____
_____

PRAYER REQUEST

_____
_____
_____
_____

DAY AND DATE _____ ___/___/_____

"But if we hope for what we do not yet have, we wait for it patiently."

Romans 8:25

MY LORD, I AM THANKFUL FOR

REFLECTIONS & THOUGHTS

PRAYER REQUEST

DAY AND DATE _____ ___ / ___ / _____

"I will give thanks to you, Lord, with all my heart; I will tell of all your wonderful deeds."

Psalm 9:1

MY LORD, I AM THANKFUL FOR

_____
_____
_____
_____
_____

REFLECTIONS & THOUGHTS

_____
_____
_____
_____
_____
_____
_____
_____
_____
_____
_____

PRAYER REQUEST

_____
_____
_____
_____

DAY AND DATE _____ ___/___/____

"The Lord will fight for you; you need only to be still."

Exodus 14:14

MY LORD, I AM THANKFUL FOR

_____
_____
_____
_____
_____

REFLECTIONS & THOUGHTS

_____
_____
_____
_____
_____
_____
_____
_____
_____
_____
_____
_____
_____

PRAYER REQUEST

_____
_____
_____
_____

DAY AND DATE _____ ___/___/____

MY LORD, I AM THANKFUL FOR

_____
_____
_____
_____
_____

REFLECTIONS & THOUGHTS

_____
_____
_____
_____
_____
_____
_____
_____
_____
_____
_____

PRAYER REQUEST

_____
_____
_____
_____
_____

DAY AND DATE _____ ___/___/_____

MY LORD, I AM THANKFUL FOR

_____

_____

_____

_____

_____

REFLECTIONS & THOUGHTS

_____

_____

_____

_____

_____

_____

_____

_____

_____

_____

_____

_____

PRAYER REQUEST

_____

_____

_____

_____

DAY AND DATE _____ ___/___/_____

MY LORD, I AM THANKFUL FOR

_____
_____
_____
_____
_____

REFLECTIONS & THOUGHTS

_____
_____
_____
_____
_____
_____
_____
_____
_____
_____
_____

PRAYER REQUEST

_____
_____
_____
_____

DAY AND DATE _____ __/__/____

"A gentle answer turns away wrath, but a harsh word stirs up anger."

Proverbs 15:1

MY LORD, I AM THANKFUL FOR

_____
_____
_____
_____
_____

REFLECTIONS & THOUGHTS

_____
_____
_____
_____
_____
_____
_____
_____
_____
_____
_____
_____

PRAYER REQUEST

_____
_____
_____
_____

DAY AND DATE _____ ___ / ___ / ____

"Be still before the Lord and wait patiently for him; do not fret when people
succeed in their ways, when they carry out their wicked schemes."

Psalm 37:7

MY LORD, I AM THANKFUL FOR

_____
_____
_____
_____
_____

REFLECTIONS & THOUGHTS

_____
_____
_____
_____
_____
_____
_____
_____
_____
_____
_____

PRAYER REQUEST

_____
_____
_____
_____
_____

"But you, man of God, flee from all this, and pursue righteousness, godliness, faith, love, endurance and gentleness."

1 Timothy 6:11

MY LORD, I AM THANKFUL FOR

REFLECTIONS & THOUGHTS

PRAYER REQUEST

DAY AND DATE _____ ___/___/_____

"As a father has compassion on his children, so the Lord has compassion on those who fear him."

Psalm 103:13

MY LORD, I AM THANKFUL FOR

_____
_____
_____
_____
_____

REFLECTIONS & THOUGHTS

_____
_____
_____
_____
_____
_____
_____
_____
_____
_____
_____
_____

PRAYER REQUEST

_____
_____
_____
_____
_____

"Rejoice in the Lord always. I will say it again: Rejoice!"

Philippians 4:4

MY LORD, I AM THANKFUL FOR

_____

_____

_____

_____

_____

REFLECTIONS & THOUGHTS

_____

_____

_____

_____

_____

_____

_____

_____

_____

_____

_____

_____

PRAYER REQUEST

_____

_____

_____

_____

DAY AND DATE _____ ___ / ___ / ___

"Commit to the Lord whatever you do, and he will establish your plans."

Proverbs 16:3

MY LORD, I AM THANKFUL FOR

REFLECTIONS & THOUGHTS

PRAYER REQUEST

"When you pass through the waters, I will be with you; and when you pass through the rivers, they will not sweep over you. When you walk through the fire, you will not be burned; the flames will not set you ablaze."

Isaiah 43:2

MY LORD, I AM THANKFUL FOR

_____
_____
_____
_____

REFLECTIONS & THOUGHTS

_____
_____
_____
_____
_____
_____
_____
_____
_____
_____
_____

PRAYER REQUEST

_____
_____
_____
_____

DAY AND DATE _____ ___/___/_____

"My salvation and my honor depend on God; he is my mighty rock, my refuge."

Psalm 62:7

MY LORD, I AM THANKFUL FOR

_____
_____
_____
_____

REFLECTIONS & THOUGHTS

_____
_____
_____
_____
_____
_____
_____
_____
_____
_____
_____

PRAYER REQUEST

_____
_____
_____
_____

DAY AND DATE _____ ___/___/_____

"Keep your lives free from the love of money and be content with what you have, because God has said, "Never will I leave you; never will I forsake you."

Hebrews 13:5

MY LORD, I AM THANKFUL FOR

_____
_____
_____
_____
_____

REFLECTIONS & THOUGHTS

_____
_____
_____
_____
_____
_____
_____
_____
_____
_____
_____
_____

PRAYER REQUEST

_____
_____
_____
_____

DAY AND DATE _____ ___/___/_____

MY LORD, I AM THANKFUL FOR

_____
_____
_____
_____
_____

REFLECTIONS & THOUGHTS

_____
_____
_____
_____
_____
_____
_____
_____
_____
_____
_____

PRAYER REQUEST

_____
_____
_____
_____
_____

"You will keep in perfect peace those whose minds are steadfast, because they trust in you."

Isaiah 26:3

MY LORD, I AM THANKFUL FOR

_____
_____
_____
_____
_____

REFLECTIONS & THOUGHTS

_____
_____
_____
_____
_____
_____
_____
_____
_____
_____
_____

PRAYER REQUEST

_____
_____
_____
_____

DAY AND DATE _____ ___/___/___

MY LORD, I AM THANKFUL FOR

_____
_____
_____
_____
_____

REFLECTIONS & THOUGHTS

_____
_____
_____
_____
_____
_____
_____
_____
_____
_____
_____
_____

PRAYER REQUEST

_____
_____
_____
_____

DAY AND DATE _____ ___/___/___

MY LORD, I AM THANKFUL FOR

_____

_____

_____

_____

_____

REFLECTIONS & THOUGHTS

_____

_____

_____

_____

_____

_____

_____

_____

_____

_____

_____

_____

PRAYER REQUEST

_____

_____

_____

_____

DAY AND DATE _____ ___ / ___ / ____

"But Scripture has locked up everything under the control of sin, so that what was promised, being given through faith in Jesus Christ, might be given to those who believe."

Galatians 3:22

MY LORD, I AM THANKFUL FOR

_____
_____
_____
_____
_____

REFLECTIONS & THOUGHTS

_____
_____
_____
_____
_____
_____
_____
_____
_____
_____
_____
_____

PRAYER REQUEST

_____
_____
_____
_____
_____

DAY AND DATE _____ ___/___/_____

"And now, dear children, continue in him, so that when he appears we may
be confident and unashamed before him at his coming."

1 John 2:28

MY LORD, I AM THANKFUL FOR

REFLECTIONS & THOUGHTS

PRAYER REQUEST

DAY AND DATE _____ ____/____/____

MY LORD, I AM THANKFUL FOR

_____

_____

_____

_____

_____

REFLECTIONS & THOUGHTS

_____

_____

_____

_____

_____

_____

_____

_____

_____

_____

_____

_____

PRAYER REQUEST

_____

_____

_____

_____

DAY AND DATE _____ ___/___/____

MY LORD, I AM THANKFUL FOR

REFLECTIONS & THOUGHTS

PRAYER REQUEST

DAY AND DATE _____ ___/___/____

"So you also must be ready, because the Son of Man will come at an hour when you do not expect him."

Matthew 24:44

MY LORD, I AM THANKFUL FOR

_____
_____
_____
_____
_____

REFLECTIONS & THOUGHTS

_____
_____
_____
_____
_____
_____
_____
_____
_____
_____
_____

PRAYER REQUEST

_____
_____
_____
_____

DAY AND DATE _____ ___/___/____

MY LORD, I AM THANKFUL FOR

_____
_____
_____
_____
_____

REFLECTIONS & THOUGHTS

_____
_____
_____
_____
_____
_____
_____
_____
_____
_____
_____

PRAYER REQUEST

_____
_____
_____
_____

DAY AND DATE _____ ___ / ___ / ___

"I am the Alpha and the Omega," says the Lord God, "who is, and who was, and who is to come, the Almighty."

MY LORD, I AM THANKFUL FOR

_____
_____
_____
_____
_____

REFLECTIONS & THOUGHTS

_____
_____
_____
_____
_____
_____
_____
_____
_____
_____
_____

PRAYER REQUEST

_____
_____
_____
_____

DAY AND DATE _____ ___/___/_____

"But many who are first will be last, and many who are last will be first."

MY LORD, I AM THANKFUL FOR

_____
_____
_____
_____
_____

REFLECTIONS & THOUGHTS

_____
_____
_____
_____
_____
_____
_____
_____
_____
_____
_____
_____
_____

PRAYER REQUEST

_____
_____
_____
_____

"Rejoice always, pray continually, give thanks in all circumstances; for this is God's will for you in Christ Jesus."

1 Thessalonians 5:16-18

MY LORD, I AM THANKFUL FOR

REFLECTIONS & THOUGHTS

PRAYER REQUEST

DAY AND DATE _____ ___/___/____

MY LORD, I AM THANKFUL FOR

REFLECTIONS & THOUGHTS

PRAYER REQUEST

DAY AND DATE _____ ___ / ___ / _____

And he took bread, gave thanks and broke it, and gave it to them, saying,
"This is my body given for you; do this in remembrance of me."

Luke 22:19

MY LORD, I AM THANKFUL FOR

_____
_____
_____
_____
_____

REFLECTIONS & THOUGHTS

_____
_____
_____
_____
_____
_____
_____
_____
_____
_____
_____

PRAYER REQUEST

_____
_____
_____
_____

YOUR GIFT

SCAN THE CODE WITH YOUR PHONE'S CAMERA

MY THOUGHTS

MY THOUGHTS

MY THOUGHTS

MY THOUGHTS

MY THOUGHTS

MY THOUGHTS

MY THOUGHTS

MY THOUGHTS

MY THOUGHTS

MY THOUGHTS

MY THOUGHTS

MY THOUGHTS

MY THOUGHTS

MY THOUGHTS

Made in the USA
Columbia, SC
03 May 2022

59893573R00122